Johann
PACHELBEL

TWO TRIO SUITES

in C Major and Bb Major

FOR TWO VIOLINS AND BASSO CONTINUO (CELLO)

K 04776

Two Trio Suites
PARTIA V

JOH. PACHELBEL

Sonata

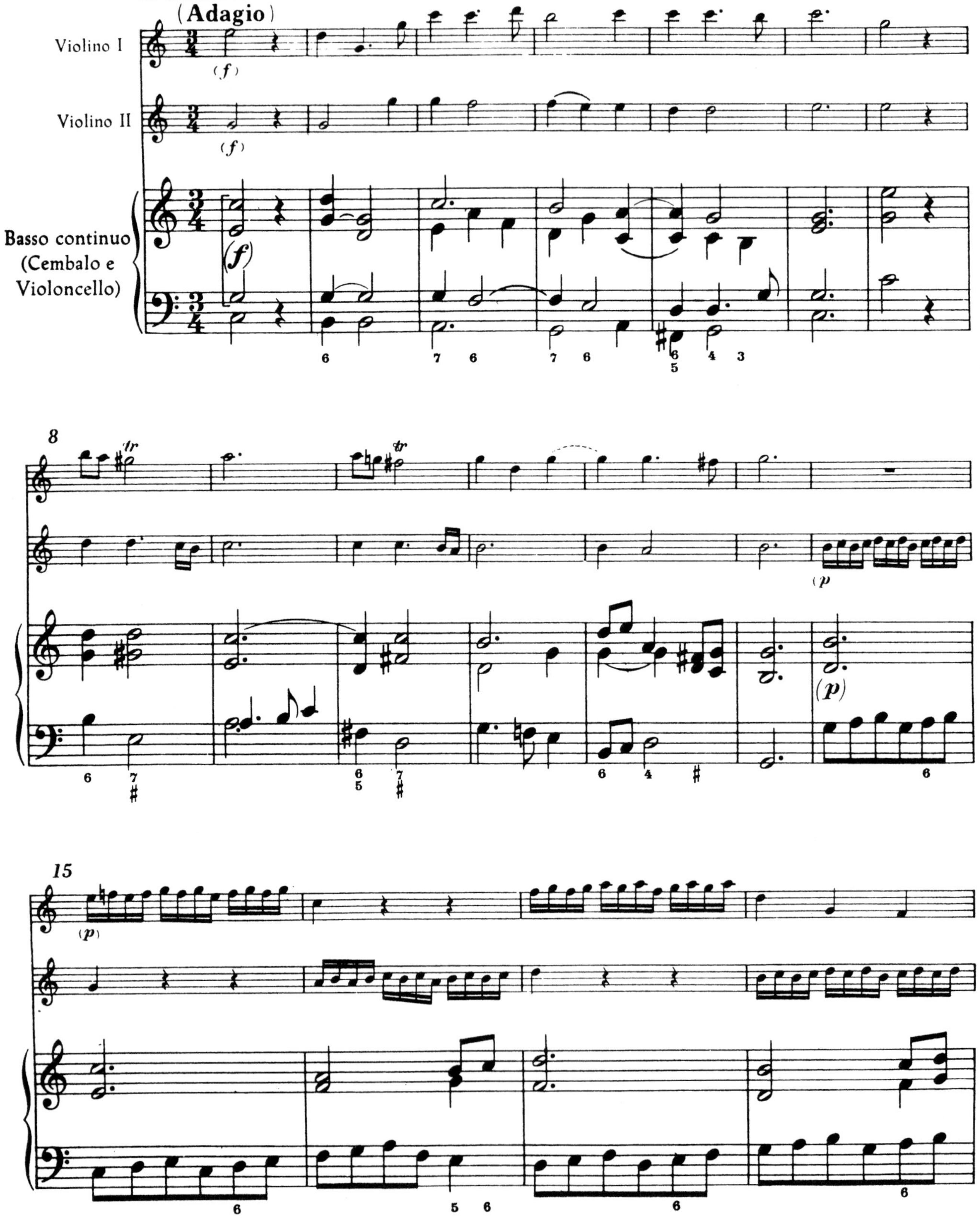

19
3
(mf)
(mf)
(mf)
7 6
6
6
6
23
6
6
7
5
6
27
(tr)
6
5
4 3
31
(f)
(f)
(f)
6
7 6
7 6
6
5
4 3

Aria

Treza

Ciacona

PARTIA VI

Sonata
JOH. PACHELBEL
Adagio
Violino I
Violino II
Basso continuo
(Cembalo e
Violoncello)
Aria

Courant

9
mf
(mf)
(mf)
6
7 6 6 6 4
5
6
13
tr.
cresc.
(f)
(cresc.)
f
(cresc.)
(f)
6 4 3
6 6
6 4 3

Gavotte

(mf)
(cresc.)
(p)
(mf)
(cresc.)
(p)
(mf)
(cresc.)
(p)
5 6 6 6 5 6 6
5
6 7 7
7
(mf)
(f)
(mf)
(f)
(mf)
(f)
6 5 6 4 5 6 6 5 6 5 6 5
2
6 4 3

Variatio

Saraband

Gigue

(f)
(mf)
(p)
(mf)
(p)
(mf)
(cresc.)
(cresc.)
(f)
(f)
(f)

19
(f)
(mf)
(f)
(mf)
(f)
(f)
6
24
(f)
(mf)
5 6 6 6 6 7 6 6 5 6
4 3
28
(f)
(mf)
(mf)
tr
(mf)
(f)
6 3 5
5
33
[cresc.]
(f)
(tr)
[cresc.]
(f)
6 6 4 6 7 6 6 4 3
2 5 4
2